TO A CHOSEN GENERATION

HARTMAN RECTOR, JR.

Bookcraft
Salt Lake City, Utah

Library of Congress Catalog Card Number: 85-71427
ISBN 0-88494-564-2

3rd Printing, 1987

Printed in the United States of America

PREFACE

As I have traveled about the Church for the past seventeen years and taught early morning seminary for five years previous to that, I have been tremendously impressed with the rising generation of young people whom the Lord has reserved for this day. They have ability and desire that will allow them to move the Church forward in its decreed destiny, to prepare a people ready to receive the Master when he comes in his glory. They are truly the youth of the noble birthright.

However, for the most part the youth do not know how or why they are chosen, and because the forces of evil are organized and arrayed in great strength and power against the progress of the Church and kingdom of God on earth, youth many times are distracted and deterred from the course they must travel.

This book is prepared to provide a few simple but very effective aids to help keep this chosen generation on course—or help them get back on course, as the case may be. It is the product of my own experience and is in no way endorsed by the Church. Specifically, if there are errors in this work, the Church and its leaders are completely absolved from the responsibility for such errors.

It is written with much love to a chosen generation.

CONTENTS

TO A CHOSEN GENERATION

"Could it be that everyone who has a body of flesh and blood earned that great blessing in his premortal life by accepting the plan of salvation and following the Master in that sphere?"

My young friend, you who are one of the "chosen" generation, have you ever wondered *why* you have been chosen? May I suggest to you that you were chosen to be a part of this generation because of your greatness. Perhaps the Prophet Joseph Smith was contemplating something of this kind when he said, "Every man who has a calling to minister to the inhabitants of the world was ordained to that purpose in the Grand Council of heaven before this world was" (*Teachings of the Prophet Joseph Smith*, compiled by Joseph Fielding Smith [Salt Lake City: Deseret Book Co., 1976], p. 365). This sounds for all the world as if many things, certainly our callings to render service to our fellowmen, were planned prior to our coming to this earth. You were chosen before you were born. Alma seemed to confirm this "premortal choosing" when he explained the calling of certain priests:

And those priests were ordained after the order of his Son. . . .

And this is the manner after which they were ordained—being called and prepared from the foundation of the world according to the foreknowledge of God, on account of their exceeding faith and good works; in the first place being left to choose good or evil; therefore they having chosen good, and exercising exceedingly great faith, are called with a holy calling. . . .

And thus they have been called to this holy calling on account of their faith, while others would reject the Spirit of God on account of the hardness of their hearts and blindness of their minds, while, if it had not been for this they might have had as great privilege as their brethren.

Or in fine, in the first place they were on the same standing with their brethren; thus this holy calling being prepared from the foundation of the world for such as would not harden their hearts, being in and through the atonement of the Only Begotten Son. (Alma 13:2–5.)

Could it be that everyone who has a body of flesh and blood earned that great blessing in his premortal life by accepting the plan of salvation and following the Master in that sphere? Jesus was the great general there. He was the leader of the forces of righteousness, and we were faithful followers. Of course, as in all conflict, the soldiers involved were permitted considerable latitude to act on their own initiative—they were not commanded in all things. Those who proved faithful were permitted to move into the next estate and receive a body of flesh and bones. Those who were not faithful followers of the Lord Jesus Christ and his generals, but on the contrary followed Lucifer, were not permitted the second estate of mortality.

There seems to be much evidence in the scriptures to indicate precisely this, which means that everyone you see in mortality (with a body of flesh and blood) has already accepted the gospel plan once, before he or she was born. All that really should be required to bring people into the Church would be to get their attention and recall to their memory that which they already know but have forgotten because of the drawing of the veil at birth. It must also be that even though *all* accepted the plan, some were more valiant in the premortal existence, just as some who accept the gospel here on earth are more valiant here. Those who were more valiant there were referred to as "noble and great," as was Abraham (see Abraham 3:22).

YOUR CALLING

"You have been called out of the darkness of the world
into the marvelous light of Christ—that is,
the gospel of Jesus Christ—and you are expected
to walk in that light."

What qualifies a person to be called *great?* Perhaps the major requirement was the same in premortality as it is here on earth. In the words of the Master, "He that is greatest among you shall be your servant" (Matthew 23:11; see also Matthew 20:26–27; D&C 50:26).

It seems that true greatness in the eyes of the Lord is always associated with service to our fellowmen. Remember when the mother of James and John, the wife of Zebedee, came to Jesus trying to get him to promise high positions of reward for her sons? (See Matthew 20:20–28.) Like all mothers, she wanted to have the best for her children; this is very normal. Jesus took this occasion to teach a very important truth with respect to rewards and greatness. First, he told James and John that they didn't know what they were asking. He asked them if they were willing to (1) drink of the cup that he would drink (which probably referred to his great sacrifice for the sins of all men), and (2) be baptized with the baptism he underwent (which probably referred to his total commitment to his Father that he would be obedient in keeping His commandments). (See 2 Nephi 31:7.)

James and John readily agreed to these conditions, probably not really having a full understanding of what they were agreeing to do. The Savior then told them that even after they had done their all they may not get the reward they were seeking—because it was not his to give. In other words, we don't serve the Lord (which really means serve our fellowmen) just because we want to receive a reward for our service. If we do, the motive is wrong, and, in the words of T. S. Eliot, "The last temptation is the greatest treason; to do the right deed for the wrong reason" (*Murder in the Cathedral*). It seems that rewards come only when we do the right things for the right reasons. In this instance, the right reason for serving our fellowmen is because we love them and love our Heavenly Father.

Even good gifts, if they are given begrudgingly, are unacceptable to the Lord and bring no reward of blessings. On the contrary, such a gift causes the giver to be accounted evil before God (see Moroni 7:6–10). After the Master had explained to James and John that he could not grant their request, he continued by telling them, "Whosoever will be great among you, let him be your minister; and whosoever will be chief among you, let him be your servant: even as the Son of man [Christ] came not to be ministered unto, but to minister, and to give his life a ransom for many" (Matthew 20:26–28).

GREATNESS EQUATES WITH SERVICE

Greatness, then, seems to grow out of unselfish service or giving of yourself. In the words of the poet, "Who gives himself with his alms feeds three, Himself, his hungering neighbor, and me [*me* meaning Christ]" (James Russell Lowell, *Vision of Sir Launfall*). As a member of this chosen generation, one of the things you are chosen to do is to render a vital service to your fellowmen. From the words in Alma 13:2–6 it appears that your chosen status was determined before you were born, as was true of Abraham and Jeremiah and many others of whom we have record. In fact, a close reading of Abraham 3:22–25 seems to indicate that this applies to all those who accept the gospel and become anxiously engaged in rendering such soul-saving service.

> *Now the Lord had shown unto me, Abraham, the intelligences that were organized before the world was; and among all these there were many of the noble and great ones;*
>
> *And God saw these souls that they were good, and he stood in the midst of them, and he said: These I will make my rulers; for he stood among those that were spirits, and he said unto me: Abraham, thou art one of them; thou wast chosen before thou wast born.*
>
> *And there stood one among them that was like unto God,*

and he said unto those who were with him: We will go down, for there is space there, and we will take of these materials, and we will make an earth whereon these [meaning all of our Heavenly Father's faithful children] may dwell;

And we will prove them herewith, to see if they will do all things whatsoever the Lord their God shall command them. (Abraham 3:22–25; emphasis added.)

Many is a relative term. When the Lord speaks of many "noble and great ones," we might ask, "Many compared to what?" If we consider the total number of people who have lived and will live on this earth—and calculated estimates place this number around sixty-eight billion so far —then *many* would mean millions and millions of people. Conceivably *many* could include everyone in every dispensation who accepts the gospel and gets involved in rendering service to his fellowmen. And "when ye are in the service of your fellow beings ye are only in the service of your God" (Mosiah 2:17). In other words—you can only serve God when you are serving your fellowmen. You can't serve God if you seclude yourself away from his children in some out-of-the-way place. You must be out among people where they can feel your love and concern for them.

It is a fact that in order to really be effective in rendering this service to our fellowmen, we must first love them. Otherwise they will not let us serve them. It has been said that people don't really care how much you know (or are willing to give) until they know how much you care.

Of course, it is easy to love people who love us. That is no problem. Right away we know they have excellent judgment. But I am not sure that we really get credit for just loving those who love us unless we can also love those who not only don't love us but don't even *like* us. Did not the Master say, "Love your enemies, bless them that curse you, do good to them that hate you, and pray for them which despitefully use you, and persecute you"? (Matthew 5:44.) I have found that we have to be very good to love people when they don't love us.

Now, the obvious question is: How do you become so good that you can love people who don't love you? Maybe if we knew why God loves *us* when we feel so unlovable most of the time, we might be able to become as he is and love everyone at all times.

GOD LOVES YOU

Did you ever wonder why God loves you?

There are two principles involved in considering the love of God for men. First, he loves all men—both the righteous and the wicked—so much that he sent his Son to open the way to the immortality and eternal life of man. Thus John wrote, "In this was manifested the love of God toward us, because that God sent his only begotten Son into the world, that we might live through him" (1 John 4:9). Jesus taught this doctrine in these words: "God so loved the world, that he gave his only begotten Son, that whosoever believeth in him should not perish, but have everlasting life'' (John 3:16).

Second, the love of God is poured out in greater abundance upon those who keep his commandments. According to his word, he loves the righteous more than he loves the wicked. ''Jacob have I loved, but Esau have I hated'' (Romans 9:13). He loves his Beloved Son, Christ, more than he loves the rebellious son of the morning, Lucifer. The thought is summarized in this Old Testament verse: ''I love them that love me; and those that seek me early shall find me'' (Proverbs 8:17).

God has given us our free agency to choose good or evil. ''Whosoever perisheth, perisheth unto himself; and whosoever doeth iniquity, doeth it unto himself; for behold, ye are free; ye are permitted to act for yourselves; for behold, God hath given unto you a knowledge and he hath made you free. He hath given unto you that ye might know good from evil, and he hath given unto you that ye might choose life or death.'' (Helaman 14:30–31.)

When we choose good, we choose God's way. This helps us become more like him and allows him to bless us, which is a manifestation of his love. Keeping his commandments is also a manifestation of our love for him, and allows us to feel his Spirit.

This special love the Lord has for his Saints, for those who keep the commandments, for those who love and serve him, is set forth in numerous New Testament passages. For instance, Jesus said: ''If ye love me, keep my commandments. . . . He that hath my commandments, and keepeth them, he it is that loveth me: and *he that loveth me shall be loved of my Father, and I will love him,* and will manifest myself unto him. . . . *If a man love me, he will keep my words: and my Father will love him.''* (John 14:15, 21, 23; italics added.)

Also: ''As the Father hath loved me, so have I loved you: *continue ye in my love. If ye keep my commandments, ye shall abide in my love;* even as I have kept my Father's commandments, and abide in his love.'' (John 15:9–10; italics added.)

Jude expressed a similar thought in these words: ''But ye, beloved, building up yourselves on your most holy faith, praying in the Holy Ghost, keep yourselves in the love of God, looking for the mercy of our Lord Jesus Christ unto eternal life'' (Jude 1:20–21).

In our day the divine word attests, ''If you keep not my commandments, the love of the Father shall not continue with you, therefore you shall walk in darkness'' (D&C 95:12).

The Lord wants us to be like him in the love he has for *all* men. In that way we abide in his love.

Ye have heard that it hath been said, Thou shalt love thy neighbor, and hate thine enemy.

But I say unto you, Love your enemies, bless them that curse you, do good to them that hate you, and pray for them which despitefully use you, and persecute you;

That ye may be the children of your father which is in heaven: for he maketh his sun to rise on the evil and on the good, and sendeth rain on the just and on the unjust.

For if ye love them which love you, what reward have ye? do not even the publicans the same?

And if ye salute your brethren only, what do ye more than others? do not even the publicans so?

Be ye therefore perfect, even as your Father which is in heaven is perfect. (Matthew 5:43–48.)

Again, how can we, you and I, become so good that we can love people who don't love us, that we may have the love of the Father continue with us? I believe that the Lord gives us a clue to this in the account of King Benjamin's last great sermon to his people in Zarahemla. The people were recounting their blessings and expressing thanks to their God "who had brought them out of the land of Jerusalem, and who had delivered them out of the hands of their enemies, and had appointed just men to be their teachers, and also a just man to be their king, who had established peace in the land of Zarahemla, and who had taught them *to keep the commandments of God, that they might rejoice and be filled with love towards God and all men*" (Mosiah 2:4; italics added).

The secret, then, is *to keep the commandments of God,* which are calculated to make us so good that we can even love those who don't love us.

CHOSEN TO BE HAPPY

There seems to be quite a lot that goes with being chosen. The Apostle Peter pointed out another of a chosen generation's specific responsibilities when he said, "But ye are a chosen generation, a royal priesthood, an holy nation, a peculiar people; that ye should shew forth the praises of him who hath called you out of darkness into his marvellous light" (1 Peter 2:9). And in D&C 29:4 the Lord goes so far as to say precisely this: "Verily, I say unto you that ye are chosen out of the world to declare my gospel with the sound of rejoicing, as with the voice of a trump." You have a responsibility to live and share the gospel.

You have been called out of the darkness of this world into the marvelous light of Christ—that is, the gospel of Jesus Christ—and you are expected to walk in that light. The darkness is so thick today that it obscures the basic purposes of life on this earth.

One basic purpose of life is to be happy. "Men are, that they might have joy" (2 Nephi 2:25). The Prophet Joseph Smith added to that statement when he said, "Happiness is the object and design of our existence; and will be the end thereof, if we pursue the path that leads to it; and this path is virtue, uprightness, faithfulness, holiness, and keeping all the commandments of God" (*Teachings of the Prophet Joseph Smith*, p. 255).

There is no happiness in disobedience—there never has been and never will be. In the words of Alma, "Wickedness never was happiness" (Alma 41:10). There are those who think sin is fun—but believe me, it is not. On the contrary, sin is extremely painful. If sin were fun, the devil would be happy, because he is constantly involved in sin. But he is not happy; in fact, he is miserable. In the words of Nephi, "he seeketh that all men might be miserable like unto himself" (2 Nephi 2:27). Does that sound as if he is happy? There is no way we can be happier than he is if we do only what he does.

If we are not careful we will look for happiness in the wrong places. I presume it has always been so. Cain thought happiness would be found in material possessions. So he slew his brother Abel in order to get his brother's possessions. This was supposed to make him happy, but it did not. In fact, it made him miserable, as ill-gotten gains always do.

HAPPINESS IS BEING THANKFUL

Happiness is mostly a state of mind and is bound up in two words: *Be thankful*. We will only be happy if we are thankful for what we have. We need not be *satisfied* with what we have so that we never try to improve our lives, but we must be thankful for what we have. It really doesn't make any difference how much or how little we may have, we can still be thankful for it. This gratitude comes as we count our blessings or pause to think on the goodness of the Lord to us.

Just what are a few of *your* choice blessings?

1. You are alive upon the earth with a twenty-four-hour endowment of time each day. (No one has more than you do.)
2. You have a marvelously formed body of flesh and bone to house and protect your spirit.
3. You have parents who may not be perfect, but who love you and want only the very best for you.

4. You have a mind that is capable of gathering unlimited knowledge, with marvelous recall powers.
5. You live in a land of freedom.
6. You have been guaranteed the right of life, liberty, and the pursuit of happiness (which includes the right to own and control property).
7. You are free to choose your profession, and there are schools all around to help you train your mind so you can become proficient in whatever field you choose to follow.
8. You live at a time when the gospel is on the earth in its fullness.
9. There is a living prophet of God on the earth who is charged with the responsibility to make sure you receive the truth concerning your heavenly parents, where you lived before you were born, why you are here on the earth, and where you will go when you die.
10. You have marvelous powers latent within your body so that you can reproduce after your own kind, run and not be weary, walk and not faint.

These are just a few of your almost countless blessings. You can add to the list almost daily if you are aware of what goes on around you.

The greatest blessings in life come to us freely, but if we are not careful we will miss them altogether by looking beyond the mark. In the words of the poet:

> *Earth gets its price from what earth gives us.*
> *The beggar is taxed for a corner to die in.*
> *We bargain for the graves we lie in.*

At the devil's booth are all things sold,
Each ounce of dross costs its ounce of gold.
For a cap and bells our lives we pay,
Bubbles we buy with a whole soul's tasking:
'Tis heaven alone that is given away,
'Tis only God may be had for the asking . . . ,
No price is set on the lavish summer,
June may be had by the poorest comer.

> (James Russell Lowell,
> "The Vision of Sir Launfal")

We miss out on many choice blessings by wishing for circumstances to change. We can't enjoy the beautiful sunshine because we want snow so we can ski. We can't enjoy the gentle falling rain because we want to "lay out" and get a suntan. We destroy our present peace by not being thankful for what we have right now.

Another important truth is that we have to be "on the way" to fulfilling our potential in order to know happiness. Happiness can only come as we feel good about ourselves. We will never be happy if we break the commandments which we know are true, for it is a fact that we will reap what we sow. If we sow disobedience, we will reap the fruits of disobedience. If we sow obedience, we will reap the rewards of obedience.

No one can be happy and fail. We are all basically winners. We have known success prior to this earth life; as offspring of God we are "programmed" for success. We came to this earth as lovable and capable beings. As we live up to our potential, as we become increasingly like our Heavenly Father, we are succeeding.

God our Heavenly Father is all-powerful in heaven and on earth (see Matthew 28:18). That is because he does everything right, and always has. He is not constantly having to redo things that were done wrong the first time. That is what takes our time and destroys our peace and efficiency: we are constantly making mistakes, and we must tear down the faulty superstructure and rebuild on a firm, correct foundation. It is like taking a wrong turn on a cross-country trip. We might do this through carelessness (not paying attention), or by honest mistakes (we thought this was the way we should go), or because we were misled by someone we trusted. But the results are always the same. When we determine that we are not getting to where we want to be, we have to stop, turn around, and retrace our steps until we return to the point where we went wrong. Time is lost, distance is lost, and energy is wasted. However, there is always a plus that can come from the mistake. We can profit by the experience. We can learn something that will preclude our making the same mistake again. "Know thou . . . that all these things shall give thee experience" (D&C 122:7).

It is just smart to do things God's way. Alma indicated that "every man receiveth wages of him whom he listeth to obey" (Alma 3:27). That means that if you follow the Lord you receive your reward from the Lord, and that is about as well as you can do, since he (the Lord) owns everything. If you follow the devil you will have to get your reward from the devil, and he doesn't own anything. All he has to share is misery. If you "do your own thing" you will have to reward yourself. How much do you own? Obviously, then, it is wise to follow the Lord, who owns the earth and everything that is in it. In the words of the Psalmist, "The earth is the Lord's, and the fulness thereof; the world, and they that dwell therein" (Psalm 24:1).

That means that we belong to the Lord, too—and that is true. "Ye are bought with a price" (1 Corinthians 6:20). The Lord has paid for our sins, and we are indebted to him for our redemption, also for the fact that we can breathe, see, walk, talk, feel, think, smell, and do according to our own will (see Mosiah 2:21). As we learn to submit our wills to his, through our obedience, we will experience the greatest happiness.

Ultimate victory is ultimate happiness. The ultimate success achievement is eternal life, wherein we have power to procreate after our own kind eternally—in very essence, to be like God. Obviously, we can't achieve this status through failure. Failure brings great sorrow and distress and despair—all of which come because of iniquity or failure to keep the commandments. Man reaches his highest and most glorious potential as he lives in obedience to God's laws. If we are not happy, we need to check our obedience level and make the proper corrections. It all boils down to whether we are keeping basic commandments—which we absolutely must do if we are to feel good about ourselves.

THE POWER OF PRAYER

In order to keep the Lord's commandments, which are only calculated to make us happy and thus are for our eternal benefit, we must know what those commandments are. Of course, we can take the word of someone else, but it is much better and much more satisfying to read the Lord's word for ourselves. Never in the history of this world have the scriptures been so readily available. Therefore, regular study of the scriptures, the recorded word of God, is within reach of everyone of us. In addition, the standard works as well as many enlightening commentaries about the scriptures are available on cassette tapes that can go with us almost anywhere. It has never been easier to study God's words to us, his children.

Just how important are the scriptures, anyway? In the first place, the scriptures were given by inspiration of God. They are his words to us through his prophets. When we read the scriptures, we literally read God's words. As the Lord has explained:

> *And I, Jesus Christ, your Lord and your God, have spoken it.*
> *These words are not of men nor of man, but of me; wherefore,*
> *you shall testify they are of me and not of man;*
> *For it is my voice which speaketh them unto you; for they are*
> *given by my spirit unto you, and by my power you can read them*

*one to another; and save it were by my power you could not have
them;*

*Wherefore, you can testify that you have heard my voice, and
know my words. (D&C 18:33–36.)*

Thus, in very deed, when you read the scriptures you
are hearing the voice of God.

Second, the scriptures are "profitable for doctrine, for
reproof, for correction, for instruction in righteousness:
that the man of God may be perfect, throughly furnished
unto all good works" (2 Timothy 3:16–17). A brief
discussion of these principles might be valuable.

The scriptures are *profitable for doctrine.* The term *doctrine* refers to the basic beliefs of the Church, the foundation upon which the Church is built. We will never really
understand the Church—or the Lord, for that
matter—until we understand the doctrine. We learn the
doctrine by reading and studying the scriptures.

The scriptures will *reprove* us when we err in our way of
life. They will straighten out our thinking when we are
misled.

The scriptures are the surest manual of *instruction in
righteousness.* There is a great deal of the wisdom of men
available today. The theories of men abound in books and
lectures on all sides. It seems that no one really knows anything for sure; people seem always to be propounding or
advancing their own theories. The scriptures stand as a
beacon light to which all can go in safety. In the words of
President Harold B Lee:

*All that we teach in this Church ought to be couched in the
scriptures. We ought to choose our texts from the scriptures. If
we want to measure truth, we should measure it by the four stan-*

*dard works, regardless of who writes it. If it is not in the standard works, we may well assume that it is speculation, man's own personal opinion; and if it contradicts what is in the scriptures it is not true. This is the standard by which we measure all truth. . . . Through these generations the messages from our Father have been safeguarded and carefully protected, and mark you likewise that in this day the scriptures are the purest at their source, just as the waters were purest at the mountain source; the purest word of God, and that least apt to be polluted, is that which comes from the lips of the living prophets who are set up to guide Israel in our own day and time. (*Ye Are the Light of the World [Salt Lake City: Deseret Book Company, 1974], pp. 55–56.)*

The scriptures admonish us also in our conduct. For instance, we are commanded to pray always, without ceasing.

Therefore may God grant unto you . . . that ye may begin to exercise your faith unto repentance, that ye begin to call upon his holy name. . . .

Yea, cry unto him for mercy; for he is mighty to save.

Yea, humble yourselves, and continue in prayer unto him.

Cry unto him when ye are in your fields [or where you work], yea, over all your flocks.

Cry unto him in your houses, yea, over all your household, both morning, mid-day, and evening.

Yea, cry unto him against the power of your enemies.

Yea, cry unto him against the devil, who is an enemy to all righteousness.

Cry unto him over the crops of your fields, that ye may prosper in them.

Cry over the flocks of your fields, that they may increase.

But this is not all; ye must pour out your souls in your closets, and your secret places, and in your wilderness.

*Yea, and when you do not cry unto the Lord, let your hearts
be full, drawn out in prayer unto him continually for your
welfare, and also for the welfare of those who are around you.
(Alma 34:17–27.)*

After reading this, one can have little doubt about the
need to pray. However, it is a fact that someone else is always listening in, and many times he tries to give us
answers. A key to detecting the devil is to remember that
he is a liar.

Satan says such things as, "One time won't hurt anything; try it, you'll like it." Have you ever heard anything
that sounded like that? One time won't hurt anything!
Why, one time can cost you your eternal exaltation. There
are no alcoholics that didn't start by taking *one* drink.
There are no drug addicts that didn't start with one
"fix." The most obvious example would be to just kill
someone one time and see how you fare.

But the devil always follows up this first lie with another
one, even more enticing. "Besides," he says, "everyone is
doing it." Maybe too many are doing it, but not *everyone* is
doing it. Only those who are deceived or are on their way
to hell are doing it. (And you may rest assured, no one
enjoys hell. Not even the devil enjoys hell. He runs the
place, but he doesn't enjoy it.)

Here is another of the devil's lies: "Anyway, no one will
ever know. It's a secret; we'll do it in the dark." Surely he
would like you to believe that no one will ever know, but
that is just another one of his lies. Obviously, the Lord
knows, and if he knows it doesn't make any difference who
else knows. Do you know what the Lord says about this?
The Lord says, "Their iniquities shall be spoken upon the

housetops, and their secret acts shall be revealed'' (D&C 1:3). Does that sound as if no one will ever know?

We must not be taken in by any of Lucifer's lies. If you know what the Lord has said in the scriptures you will not be deceived, and unless you do know what the Lord has said, you most certainly will be deceived.

TIMES WILL WORSEN

We are living on the earth at a very difficult time. Physical requirements are not particularly demanding—in fact, they are nothing compared with what existed just sixty years ago. However, the spiritual wickedness of many in high places presents a challenge to us today that has seldom if ever been experienced on this earth. Perhaps the period just before the flood may have been worse than our time; Moses recorded of those days that "the wickedness of man was great in the earth, and that every imagination of the thoughts of his heart was only evil continually" (Genesis 6:5). I have never known anyone quite so bad that they never had a good thought, but we can be assured that this condition will surely exist again prior to the second coming of the Master. But as the days of Noah were, so shall the coming of the Son of man be (see Matthew 24:37; see also Luke 17:26).

Paul gave some specifics as to just what would be happening at that time. He said:

> *This know also, that in the last days perilous times shall come.*
>
> *For men shall be lovers of their own selves, covetous, boasters, proud, blasphemers, disobedient to parents, unthankful, unholy.*
>
> *Without natural affection, trucebreakers, false accusers, incontinent, fierce, despisers of those that are good,*
>
> *Traitors, heady, highminded, lovers of pleasures more than lovers of God;*
>
> *Having a form of godliness; but denying the power thereof: from such turn away.*
>
> *For of this sort are they which creep into houses, and lead captive silly women laden with sins, led away with divers lusts,*
>
> *Ever learning, and never able to come to the knowledge of the truth. . . .*
>
> *Yea, and all that will live godly in Christ Jesus shall suffer persecution.*
>
> *But evil men and seducers shall wax worse and worse, deceiving, and being deceived.*
>
> *But continue thou in the things which thou hast learned and hast been assured of, knowing of whom thou hast learned them;*
>
> *And that from a child thou hast known the holy scriptures, which are able to make thee wise unto salvation through faith which is in Christ Jesus. (2 Timothy 3:1–7, 12–15.)*

Paul indicates that all that will live godly in Christ will suffer persecution. Yes! Living upon the earth is a great privilege—however, it is fraught with danger. This is our testing time, a time of probation. In order for the testing to be effective, there had to be commandments given, the violation of which would bring upon us the judgment of God.

YOUR MISSION

"Happiness is mostly victory. . . . Real happiness
comes as we successfully fulfill our mission to
'raise a family in the Lord.'"

The first great overarching and undergirding commandment was to "be fruitful, and multiply and replenish the earth." Why? I'm sure our first parents wanted to know.

The answer: That we might have joy and rejoicing in our posterity, or so that we would be happy. Joy and happiness are at the root of every commandment that God our Father has given us. Joy was the purpose of our creation.

What, then, will make us happy? Successfully fulfilling our mission here in mortality. Remember? Happiness is not mostly pleasure. Happiness is mostly victory. We have to be successful to be happy. Real happiness comes as we successfully fulfill our mission to "raise a family in the Lord," for that is what the Lord's commandment to our first parents in the Garden of Eden really meant. "Be fruitful, multiply and replenish the earth," he said. That means we must bear and nurture God's spirit children in mortality and teach them to love him, obey him, and walk uprightly before him. That is the only way they (our children) can be happy, and if they are not happy we as their parents will not be happy either. I have never seen unhappy children that had happy parents. I'm sure they don't exist. Your happiness will be inseparably connected with the happiness of your children.

Therefore, if you will fulfill your destiny as a youth of the noble birthright—those who are called out of darkness into the marvelous light of Christ—in that you insist on raising a large family in the Lord at this time in history when large families are becoming unpopular, you will probably be required to pay more maternity costs, face discrimination in public housing, lose tax benefits, and deal with a host of other obstacles designed to discourage large families. This is already happening in some countries in the world today. The family planners and birth-control advocates will have power. However, you are here to fulfill your mission and raise a family in the Lord. In order to do this you must keep in mind four fundamental principles:

1. You must be married in the temple.
2. You must provide for your family.
3. You must have your children when you can.
4. You must raise your children in the Church.

Perhaps a discussion of these four basic principles would be profitable so that we might better understand what the Lord expects of us.

TEMPLE MARRIAGE

One—you must be married in the temple. Why? Because if you raise a family without being sealed in the temple the day will come when you will surely lose your family and you will fail in your mission. Hear the words of the Lord on the subject:

> *All covenants, contracts, bonds, obligations, oaths, vows, performances, connections, associations, or expectations, that are not made and entered into and sealed by the Holy Spirit of promise, of him who is anointed, both as well for time and for all eternity, and that too most holy, by revelation and commandment through the medium of mine anointed, whom I have appointed on the earth to hold this power (and I have appointed unto my servant Joseph to hold this power in the last days, and there is never but one on the earth at a time on whom this power and the keys of this priesthood are conferred), are of no efficacy, virtue, or force in and after the resurrection from the dead; for all contracts that are not made unto this end have an end when men are dead (D&C 132:7).*

Therefore, you must be married in the temple. In order to be married in the temple, you must receive a temple recommend. In order to receive a temple recommend, you must pass a very detailed and pointed interview with your bishop and stake president. They will want to know basically two things: (1) Are you honest? (2) Are you morally clean?

Temptation and Honesty

All the questions you will be asked are concerned with these two principles. The first, honesty, is fundamental to your exaltation. It isn't a question of whether we believe in honesty; almost everybody does. Mohandas K. Gandhi once said, "There are ninety-nine men who believe in honesty for every honest man." We all believe in honesty, but are we really honest?

Are we honest in little things? Generally speaking, most of us don't have any real problems with big dishonest acts. For instance, do you know anyone who has a problem with robbing banks? You see? We don't usually start with large dishonest acts, but with much smaller ones. A more difficult question might be, Did you ever cheat on a test in school? That is where dishonesty flowers and blooms.

I had a good friend, a returned missionary, who was attending Brigham Young University. He reported that at one time he attended a class in which a test was scheduled, but he had not studied for the test and so was woefully unprepared. Of course, he had prayed fervently about this situation. But he was asking the Lord to help him remember something he had not bothered to learn. Do you suppose that the Lord could do that? Well, of course, he could—the Lord knows everything. As Nephi records, "O how great the holiness of our God! For he *knoweth all things*, and there is *not anything save he knows it.*" (2 Nephi 9:20; italics added.) Yes, the Lord could have given my friend the answers even though he had not studied, but he

(the Lord) *would not.* I know about these situations. I have
tried it, and it doesn't work that way.

When my friend arrived and was settled in the class-
room, he found he was sitting right next to the smartest girl
in the class. He said he could not help but think, "This
must be the answer to my prayer. The Lord has provided
this situation for me."

Do you suppose the Lord would do something like that?
Would he place this very smart girl next to my friend? I
believe he might. If I were the Lord, I would—not to help
him with the test, but to tempt him. It doesn't hurt to be
tempted, does it? Isn't that part of the test—to choose
between good and evil?

Well, as I said, my friend was a returned missionary. He
had been preaching honesty for two years. It is very difficult to violate a principle of which you have a testimony
—I mean a burning in your heart and mind that says, "Be
thou honest and all things will work together to your good.
You will be much further ahead by not copying from this
paper next to you than you could ever be by doing it any
other way." With that kind of a witness, it is very difficult
to cheat. So while my friend was arguing with himself, he
flunked the test—but in reality, he passed that test. You
see, he had passed the Lord's test, and that is our real test
here in mortality. Any employer would five hundred times
rather have as an employee a young man who was honest
than one who got good grades dishonestly. Would you like
to have your appendix removed by a doctor who had
cheated on his test? But when the pressure is on, the temptations are always great.

Everyone faces temptations on this earth. Even the
Master was severely tempted, as recorded in Matthew

4:2–10. Jesus had fasted for forty days and nights. Do you suppose he was hungry? There can be no doubt of it. (Just think about how difficult it is to fast for two meals.) Of course Jesus was hungry, and Satan was right there with a tempting proposition. He said to the Master, "If thou be the Son of God, command that these stones be made bread" (Matthew 2:3). That is typical of the way Lucifer works: he always attacks the weakest point. The Master was hungry; he had a physical need. The temptation was to misuse the great creative power he possessed as the Son of God to satisfy his own physical appetite. Surely the same temptation will be used on you; as offspring of God you are also endowed with great creative powers. You have the power to procreate after your own kind eternally. That is tremendous power, and the temptation will be to use this marvelous power to satisfy your own physical, selfish appetites. You can expect it.

How will you handle this diabolical threat to your eternal life? Perhaps you can handle it the same way Jesus handled it. He said, "It is written, Man shall not live by bread alone, but by every word that proceedeth out of the mouth of God" (Matthew 4:4).

The key to overcoming temptation, then, is to go right back to the scriptures. "It is written," the Master said. Where is it written? Why, in the holy scriptures, of course. Remember what Paul said? The scriptures are "for reproof, for correction, for instruction in righteousness" (2 Timothy 3:16). We can get all our answers readily from the scriptures.

This means that we must abide by the written word of God, or the standard works of the Church. These include the Bible (Old and New Testaments), the Book of Mormon: Another Testament of Jesus Christ, the Doctrine and Covenants, and the Pearl of Great Price. However, revelation goes beyond these works. In order to live by every word that proceedeth out of the mouth of God, we must follow the living prophet on earth today. If the Lord is going to make any changes in his Church, you may rest assured that they will come through his living prophet. And it is a fact that the Lord does make changes from time to time. It is also important that we follow those who serve under the direction of the living prophet, such as our stake presidents and bishops. If you live by every word that proceedeth from God you may even have to obey your parents.

Well, the devil didn't quit after his first defeat. He took the Master up on a pinnacle of the temple and said: "If thou be the Son of God, cast thyself down [why don't you jump off?]: for it is written, He shall give his angels charge concerning thee: and in their hands they shall bear thee up, lest at any time thou dash thy foot against a stone (Matthew 4:6). (It is interesting that the devil chose to quote scripture himself, but of course, he quoted it out of context, and that is lying.) The temptation here was to misuse the promises the Father had made concerning the Son—that is, that Jesus would be protected in the performance of his mission—to perform some great feat in order to get public attention. The Savior could thus have gained a following based on adoration and worship that would have resulted in power and control over many lives.

Once again Jesus had the answer: "It is written again, Thou shalt not tempt the Lord thy God." I must confess I never really understood this answer until I was married and had children of my own. Then it became clear what the Lord had said. Surely it is a great temptation for parents to protect their children from the consequences of their acts. They would like to keep them from suffering when they do something selfishly stupid.

However, if we never had to pay for our mistakes, we would never profit by our experiences. We would never learn obedience by the things which we suffer if we were never permitted to suffer. The Tyndale translation of the Bible records Jesus' answer this way, "Jesus retorted, It also says not to put the Lord your God to a foolish test" (Matthew 4:7). The Son had come to the earth to pay the price for sin, break the bonds of death, make the resurrection a reality, and open the doors of eternal life to all— a tremendously important assignment. True servants of the Lord dare not tempt God by putting him to a "foolish test." Therefore, whenever you see great religious feats being performed on television, such as healing the sick or speaking in tongues, you know from where the power is coming. It is *not* coming from the Lord. When Jesus performed such public healings, on isolated occasions, he generally told the recipients, "see thou tell no man" (see Matthew 8:4; Luke 5:14). In other words, he did not do these things before the world in order to get a following. Thus, he prevailed over the second temptation.

Then Jesus was carried in the spirit up on a great high mountain. The devil came once again and showed him all the kingdoms of the world and the glory of them, and said, "All these things will I give thee, if thou wilt fall down and worship me." Wasn't that generous of the devil, to try to give the Lord his own earth? The earth doesn't belong to the devil, it belongs to the Lord. In the words of the

Psalmist, "The earth is the Lord's, and the fulness thereof; the world, and they that dwell therein" (Psalm 24:1).

By this time Jesus must have been weary, for he said: "Get thee hence, Satan: for it is written, Thou shalt worship the Lord thy God, and him only shalt thou serve" (Matthew 4:10). The devil then left Jesus alone. This is another solid evidence that if we resist the devil he will flee from us (see James 4:7).

Our problem is that we usually listen to Satan just enough to keep his interest, so he stays after us. We wonder, "Would one cigarette really hurt? After all, I'm not a smoker, but I wonder how it tastes." "Maybe I could look at one pornographic magazine, attend one X-rated movie, or try one sip of beer." These are not grievous sins, but they do keep the devil's attention, and it would be much better if we could show him that paying attention to us is a waste of his time.

Moral Cleanliness Next to Godliness

Yes, we must be honest in overcoming temptation, and we must also be morally clean. Moral cleanliness and clean conduct begin with clean thoughts. It is a fact that the thought is the mother of the act. We become what we think about all day long. President Spencer W. Kimball has said, "How can a man possibly become what he is not thinking?" Therefore, if we are to stay clean we must keep our thoughts clean. This is not an easy task in this day and time. Pornography is everywhere we look: It is in magazines and newspapers, on the radio and television, in the movies—it is everywhere.

Someone commenting on the availability of this filth said, "You can't keep an evil thought from knocking at the door of your mind today." Someone else a little wiser said, "Yes, but you don't have to invite it in and serve it pie á la mode." We don't have to entertain evil thoughts. What we must do—and only we can do this—is get rid of evil thoughts. How? By replacing them with good thoughts. How? One way would be to quote scriptures to yourself. It is a fact that as wonderful as the human brain is, still it is unable to think of more than one thought at a time. So, if an evil thought comes into your mind, think of an inspiring passage of scripture or the words of one of our great latter-day hymns. You will find that the evil thought will be gone and you will be left to concentrate on that which is virtuous, lovely, of good report, and praise-worthy.

At this point I would like to impress upon you a vitally important, fundamental principle of the gospel: If you have made a mistake, you can repent of it. You can repent of anything except murder and the sin against the Holy Ghost. Most people will never have any problem with these things—and everything else we can repent of. How? We confess our sins and forsake them and follow the Lord. This is the crux of the gospel of Jesus Christ. To whom do we confess? To him whom we have wronged and to our bishop. It is also important that we confess to the Lord even though he already knows what we have done. He wants to know that we know, too. If we never confess the sin we will likely never forsake it, which is probably the most important part of repentance. We must also make restitution to the best of our ability to do so.

Repentance is a gift granted by the Lord Jesus Christ; without him there could be no repentance. We could be sorry and not commit the sin again, but we couldn't be forgiven. *Only* the Lord Jesus Christ could pay the price for sin. "There was no other good enough," as the hymn so clearly states ("There Is a Green Hill Far Away," *Hymns,* no. 201).

Although repentance is available, it would be much better not to have sinned in the first place. There are some excellent ways to avoid evil. One of the best is to live sufficiently above the law that you will have complete freedom through obedience to the commandment. If you constantly see how close you can walk to the edge of the cliff without falling off, your daily existence will be fraught with danger and you will know little or no security. Even the slightest slip will send you plummeting into the abyss of sin. May I illustrate from my own experience.

For twenty-six years I was privileged to fly the United States Navy's airplanes. It was very exciting to see how close I could fly to the trees without hitting them. When you are flying just above the treetops, the slightest engine malfunction or down draft in the wind would put your airplane in the trees. Let's suppose the Navy had a commandment, "Thou shalt not fly thy airplane in the trees." As a matter of fact, they did have such a commandment, and they got terribly excited if you did fly their airplane into the trees. In order for me to live free of the consequences of breaking the Navy's commandment I gave myself a commandment that was more restrictive than the Navy's. My commandment was: "Thou shalt not fly thy airplane closer than 5,000 feet to the trees." As I lived my commandment, it made living the Navy's commandment no problem at all. So it is with the Lord's commandments.

Paul seems to be recommending the same thing when he advises us to avoid even the appearance of evil (see 1 Thessalonians 5:22). What are some commandments we could profitably adopt in order to make sure we will live the Lord's law? I will suggest a few:

1. Thou shalt not enter a house alone with your date.
2. Thou shalt not ever, ever, ever enter a bedroom alone with your date.
3. Thou shalt not park on a lonely road in a potential necking and petting situation.
4. Thou shalt not attend X- or R-rated movies.
5. Thou shalt not drink cola drinks (even though it is possible to receive a temple recommend if you do).
6. Thou shalt not read or look at pornographic literature of any kind.
7. Thou shalt never accept another date with Charlie, or thou shalt never take Alice out again. (Sometimes two people are not good for each other. They just don't bring out the best in each other. In these instances it may be best not to associate together.)

I am sure you can add to this list because you know your own weaknesses. If you recognize your weaknesses and avoid temptations in those areas, the Lord will make you strong in the very things in which you are weak (see Ether 12:27). So if you have a weakness, don't despair—but don't neglect it, either. Rightly understood, it merely points out where the Lord expects you to excel. All that is required is that you come unto him. Have faith in him, confess your sins, and then follow him (by keeping his commandments), and he will make weak things become strong unto you.

If you are honest and morally clean you can receive a recommend to be married in the temple. But you can't get married or sealed in the temple by yourself. It takes two. This means you must go to the temple with someone worthy to attend the temple, and that means you should date Latter-day Saints. It is a fact of life that we marry the people we date. I'm sure there are very few times that two people, in this day and time in our society, have gotten married without dating first. And if there are instances in which two young people do get married without dating first, they probably really don't know each other. The purpose of dating is to get acquainted so that you will have some idea of whom you are marrying. It is very important to be able to communicate with your eternal companion. Talk together, do uplifting and inspiring things together. You need to be excited and feel good just to be in each other's company. If you can't get along together before you are married, you surely won't be able to communicate after you are married. You need to enjoy the same things and be considerate of each other's wants and desires.

It is also true that if you can't respect the Lord's commandments you won't respect each other. You must be honest and clean when you kneel at the altar in the temple. You see, the Lord has a way of keeping people from receiving blessings who are not worthy to receive them. Every ordinance performed on the earth must be sealed by the Holy Spirit of Promise. This is a stamp of approval that the Lord places upon an ordinance when it is (1) performed by one having authority to perform it, (2) received by one worthy to receive it, and (3) performed where and in the manner that the Lord has decreed it must be done. When these three conditions are met the Lord accepts and places his stamp of approval on the ordinance. If the couple are not worthy when they kneel at the altar, the Lord does not accept the ordinance and they are not sealed. If they were worthy when they went to the temple and then later violated their covenants, the Lord removes his acceptance, and they are no longer sealed. If they repent and become as worthy as they were when the Lord first accepted the ordinance, he will accept it again. He can accept or not accept an ordinance at anytime, but you cannot fool him. You can only fool yourself.

When you kneel at the altar of the temple you are making an eternal covenant. This means that if in the future problems develop in your marriage, the answer is not divorce—the answer is repentance on the part of both parties. As we have previously stated, a person can repent of anything except murder or the sin against the Holy Ghost. Few people have any problem with these things. Anything else you can repent of. Of course, it may take time, but you can do it; you are actually agreeing that you will repent when you make an eternal covenant. Nothing in this world is eternal without repentance. Therefore, when this covenant is consummated, you, in reality, make the Lord Jesus Christ a partner in your relationship. Without him you could not repent and become clean, and your relationship would not be eternal. So when you have made an eternal covenant with the Lord across the altar of the temple, and a problem develops in the marriage, it is time for both partners to repent. This you are agreeing to do when you make an eternal covenant—do not forget it.

PROVIDE FOR THE FAMILY

Once you have been sealed in the temple, this is not the end of your responsibilities; it is only the beginning. *The second principle* of raising a family in the Lord has to do with the father's responsibility to provide for the family. He must feed them, clothe them, shelter them, and educate them—all of which are very expensive. This means he has to have a good job, be willing to work hard, bring home everything he makes, and give it to his wife. That is called sacrifice, and it is sacrifice that brings forth the blessings of heaven.

In order for a father to secure a good job today, he must have a good education. Make whatever sacrifices are necessary to get your education, but be sure you get it. I don't mean by this that you must have a Ph.D. or a master's degree or even a bachelor's degree, unless that is what you want. If you want it, you can have it—God does grant unto men according to their desires (see Alma 29:4). Of course, there is a price that must be paid. There is always a price, but if you really want it, you can have it. However, an advanced degree is not absolutely necessary. There are excellent trade schools that can prepare a young man to earn a good living sufficient to provide for his family. Whatever avenues they pursue, it is important for fathers to accept and fulfill the responsibility of providing for their families.

In saying this to the young woman I do not mean to imply that she should not get the best education it is possible to obtain. While it is not her primary responsibility to provide for the family, conditions and circumstances many times exist that make it necessary for the wife to seek employment outside the home. It is also a fact that about 3 percent of the young women never marry. While the Church strongly recommends that mothers be home while their children are being reared, this does not preclude wives working before children grace the home or after the children have matured and left home.

BEAR THE LORD'S CHILDREN

The *third principle* of raising a family in the Lord has to do with the mother. It is the mother's responsibility to bear the children and for the most part care for them through childhood. This was plainly stated in a letter from the First Presidency to Church leaders in 1969. Perhaps it would be well to quote from that statement:

We have been commanded to multiply and replenish the earth that we may have joy and rejoicing in our posterity. . . .

Men must be considerate of their wives who bear the greater responsibility not only of bearing children, but of caring for them through childhood. *To this end the mother's health and strength should be conserved and the husband's consideration for his wife is his first duty, and self-control a dominant factor in all their relationships.*

It is our further feeling that married couples should seek inspiration and wisdom from the Lord that they may exercise discretion in solving their marital problems, and that they may be permitted to rear their children in accordance with the teachings of the gospel. (Emphasis added.)

From this statement we learn that the mother has the major responsibility not only to bear the children, but also to care for them through childhood. The husband has the responsibility to help the wife conserve her strength, and that could mean that he helps care for the children.

There is so much misinformation abroad in the land on the subject of birth control that we would do well to know that the Lord expects us to bear his children. In fact, he commands us to multiply and replenish the earth. It is true that parents cannot determine when they are going to have children. The Lord seems to control conception. Parents can determine that they are *not* going to have children, but usually they can't determine that they *are* going to have children.

Of course there are circumstances in which married couples cannot have children, and some people do not even get married. So through no fault of their own they are not able to fulfill this commandment. If that is the case, surely the Lord will accept their offering as completely as if they were able. Indeed, he has said as much:

> *Verily, verily, I say unto you, that when I give a command-ment to any of the sons of men to do a work unto my name, and those sons of men go with all their might and with all they have to perform that work, and cease not their diligence, and their enemies come upon them and hinder them from performing that work, behold, it behooveth me to require that work no more at the hands of those sons of men, but to accept of their offerings (D&C 124:49).*

May I say a word here about abortion. It is a filthy, dirty, Satan-inspired practice, but it is increasing yearly in the world and in the United States, too. For instance, abortions can be secured in some states today up through the twentieth week of pregnancy. That is five months—which means the body of a child is being destroyed. I know that it is, for I have seen children born at five months who lived and grew to maturity. This is one practice that cannot be tolerated by the Lord. President Spencer W. Kimball has stated the position of the Church on this practice as follows: "As to abortion, we deplore the reported million unborn children who will lose their lives in this country this year. Certainly the women who yield to this ugly sin and the sin which often generates it and those who assist them should remember that retribution is sure. It is sure." (*Ensign*, November 1974, p. 9.) To this could be added the official statement from the First Presidency, which says in part: "The Church opposes abortion and counsels its members not to submit to or perform an abortion except in the rare cases where, in the opinion of competent medical counsel, the life or good health of the mother is seriously endangered or where the pregnancy was caused by rape and produces serious emotional trauma in the mother. Even then it should be done only after counseling with the local priesthood authority and after receiving divine confirmation through prayer'' (*Church News,* January 27, 1973, p. 7.)

Heaven forbid that any of you sweet sisters who might read this book would ever get yourself into a condition where you would conceive a child out of wedlock. But if you do, I would strongly recommend that you have the child. Don't destroy it. You can repent of the sin of fornication—and yes, it is a sin; in fact, fornication and adultery are very grievous sins, as President Kimball has said. But you can repent of such a sin so completely that you may have the child sealed to you in the temple of the Lord. I know you can, because I have performed such sealings. But if you destroy that child, I promise you that you will never have it sealed to you. *Please* do not get involved in this Satan-inspired practice.

RAISE THEM IN THE CHURCH

The *fourth aspect* of fulfilling our mission of raising a family in the Lord is to raise them in the Church. This means for the most part that we must be *active* in the

Church. Children still walk pretty much in the footprints of their parents. Of course, there are some exceptions, but basically children still follow parents. If the parents are active, chances are good that their children will be, too.

The secret to activity in the Church is the payment of tithing. There is something about paying tithing that makes people active in the Church. So I would recommend that you always pay your tithing, and if you do you have a promise from the Lord that you will always have sufficient for your needs. You will be able to provide for all the choice spirits the Lord sees fit to send you. You will be active in the Church, raise your family in the Church, and be a great success in your mission in mortality.

Now, these are some of the main things you have to remember. There really aren't very many of them, are there? If you do these four things, you can do just about anything else in righteousness you want to do while here in mortality.

I have not mentioned everything that we are supposed to do because the list would be almost endless—just as the list of what not to do would be endless—but in the words of King Benjamin, "This much I can tell you, that if ye do not watch yourselves, and your thoughts, and your words, and your deeds, and observe the commandments of God, and continue in the faith of what ye have heard concerning the coming of our Lord, even unto the end of your lives, ye must perish. And now, O man, remember, and perish not." (Mosiah 4:30.)

REMAINING A CHOSEN GENERATION

" 'Every man gives his life for what he believes.
Every woman gives her life for what she believes. . . .
But to surrender what you are and live without belief—
that's more terrible than dying.' "

In summary, then, you must do these four things to raise a family in the Lord and fulfill your mortal mission:

First: Get married in the temple and keep yourself in condition to return there frequently to renew your covenants. If you don't, you will forget your covenants, and if you forget your covenants you will find yourself breaking them—and believe me, you will not get away with that.

Second: Brethren, get a good education so you can secure a good job and make sufficient money to provide for your family.

Third: Sisters, you must bear the children and for the most part care for them through childhood. You should bear them when you can, but not so fast

53

that you would destroy your health. As mothers you must be healthy both mentally and physically—but do not neglect to raise the Lord's children.

Fourth: Pay your tithing so you will always be active in the Church and raise your family in the Church.

If you do these four things, you will be blessed. *These things are important.*

I will close this discussion with a quotation from a play I saw at Brigham Young University some years ago titled *Joan of Lorraine.* It was the story of Joan of Arc. No doubt you know the story. A young girl heard voices she was sure came from the Lord. She followed those voices and in so doing led the armies of France to great military victories. But at the height of her military success, the tide of public opinion turned against her, and she was captured and turned over to the Catholic Church, which did not believe in revelation from the Lord. The Inquisition gave her an option. She could deny she had heard these "voices" from the Lord, and they would permit her to live—in prison. Or, if she insisted that she had heard the voices, they would burn her at the stake as a witch. Joan did not want to die. She was nineteen years old. She had everything to live for, but she was honest. She knew she had heard these voices and she knew God knew it too. She could not deny it, so she was burned at the stake as a witch. Near the close of the play, the playwright Maxwell Anderson has her say these words:

> *Every man gives his life for what he believes. Every woman gives her life for what she believes. Sometimes people believe in little or nothing. Nevertheless, they give up their lives for that*

> *little or nothing. One life is all that we have, and we live it as we believe in living it, and then it is gone. But to surrender what you are and live without belief—that's more terrible than dying—more terrible than dying young.*

Surely there are a lot of things more terrible than dying. One is to fail to live up to the high commission you received from your Heavenly Father when you were appointed to come to this earth to fill your mission in mortality. For you are truly the youth of the noble birthright—"A chosen generation, a royal priesthood, an holy nation, a peculiar people; that ye should shew forth the praises of him who hath called you out of darkness into his marvellous light" (1 Peter 2:9). The marvelous light of Christ is the gospel of Jesus Christ.

Will you be loyal to that royal which is within you? I pray that you will—in the holy name of Jesus Christ, Amen.